Original title:
Unfurling Myths Beside the Elf Hoop

Copyright © 2025 Swan Charm
All rights reserved.

Author: Liina Liblikas
ISBN HARDBACK: 978-1-80562-011-2
ISBN PAPERBACK: 978-1-80563-532-1

Echoes of Elven Laughter

In glades where sunlight weaves,
The elves dance beneath the leaves.
Their laughter rings like silver chime,
A melody lost, yet so sublime.

In meadows bright with blooms so rare,
They spin their joy upon the air.
A twirl, a leap, the magic grows,
In every heart, their mirth bestows.

With whispers soft as twilight's kiss,
They share their secrets, rich in bliss.
The rustling trees their stories tell,
Of ancient days where shadows dwell.

Each night, the stars in silence gleam,
Reflecting back their ageless dream.
In every echo, hope is found,
Where elven laughter knows no bound.

So wander forth to these pure lands,
With open heart and willing hands.
There in the quiet, find your song,
And dance where you, too, will belong.

Moonbeams and Elder Boughs

Beneath the arch of ancient trees,
Where night is stirred by gentle breeze,
The moon spills light, a silver thread,
That weaves its way where dreams are fed.

Elder boughs with stories old,
Guard secrets of the brave and bold.
They whisper to the passing night,
Of battles lost and love's sweet plight.

Each shadow casts a tale anew,
Of fairy sights and skies so blue.
With every rustle, tales ignite,
In sacred hush, the world feels right.

The stars align with secrets vast,
A tapestry of present, past.
Embrace the glow, let worries cease,
In moonlit realms, you'll find your peace.

So linger long where shadows blend,
Where nature's magic knows no end.
In twilight's grace, find solace true,
For moonbeams dance, and so should you.

The Weaving of Ethereal Tales

In twilight hours, the loom stands still,
Awaiting threads of heart and will.
With gentle hands, the weavers start,
To craft their tales with magic's art.

Each strand a dream, each knot a wish,
In every loop, the sweetest fish.
They pull the fibers, soft and bright,
To capture echoes of the night.

The tales unfold with every weave,
Of yonder worlds, of those who believe.
In shadows deep, in sunlight's glare,
The stories dance upon the air.

As stars draw near, their whispers flow,
Around the loom where wonders glow.
So gather close, let silence thrall,
For every tale invites us all.

To weave our hopes with threads so fine,
In every heart, a tale divine.
Through endless nights, our voices soar,
In the tapestry we all explore.

Timeless Whispers of the Woods

In ancient woods where shadows dwell,
Where secrets hide and echoes swell,
The whispers weave through leaves and air,
A language known to those who care.

Each step you take on mossy floor,
Will lead you to the forest's core.
With every breath, the magic hums,
In harmony, the woodland drums.

Sunlight dapples on the ground,
While solemn trees, wise and profound,
Stand sentinel through night and day,
Guarding paths where spirits play.

The brook flows clear with tales of yore,
Of childhood dreams and legends sore.
Each ripple sings, each gurgle smiles,
Inviting wanderers for miles.

So listen close, let silence guide,
Within the woods, love will abide.
In timeless whispers, truth will find,
The echoes of a gentle mind.

Murmurs of the Celestial Grove

In whispers soft, the stars align,
Beneath the boughs where moonbeams shine,
A symphony of night's embrace,
Awakens dreams in this secret place.

The rustling leaves, a hallowed tune,
Swaying gently to a silvery moon,
Each shadow dances, softly cast,
Echoes of a forgotten past.

The owls converse in hushed delight,
Guardians of the velvet night,
With wisdom wrapped in twilight's cloak,
Their voices weave, and softly evoke.

In starlit glades where fairies play,
Their laughter lights the twilight gray,
A sparkling haze of hopes and dreams,
Life flows through soft, enchanted streams.

So linger here, in nature's keep,
Where every sigh and secret weep,
Murmurs sway on the night breeze,
In Celestial Groves, hearts find ease.

The Elven Rhapsody of Lost Time

In the forest deep, where shadows twine,
Elves weave tales, in rhythm divine,
Each note a thread in time's embrace,
A rhapsody lost in a delicate space.

With silver strings, they strum the night,
Melodies that dance in soft moonlight,
Echoes of laughter, bright and clear,
A haunting tune for those who hear.

From ancient woods, the stories rise,
Of battles bold and whispered lies,
They sing of love both fierce and bright,
And all the dreams that fade from sight.

In twilight's glow, their voices soar,
A harmony that stirs the core,
Of memories sweet, both lost and found,
In melodies spun from nature's sound.

So come, dear friend, and listen near,
To rhapsodies that hold you dear,
Where every note, like time entwined,
Awakens the myths of heart and mind.

Sighs of the Enchanted Thicket

In tangled vines where secrets dwell,
The thicket sighs, a magic spell,
With every breath, a tale unfolds,
Of ancient paths, and whispers bold.

Soft light filters through leafy skies,
A dance of shadows and gentle sighs,
The guardians of the thicket know,
The stories hidden where no winds blow.

With echoes low, the branches sway,
As if to beckon the weary stay,
In this realm where dreams collide,
Each sigh a door, the heart's true guide.

Among the thorns, the blossoms bloom,
Creating beauty from whispered gloom,
The fragrant air, a soothing balm,
In enchanted thicket, all is calm.

So wander deep, let worries cease,
In rustling leaves, find your peace,
Where every sigh, and every hue,
Brings forth the magic hidden from view.

Fables Woven in Nature's Embrace

In a tapestry of emerald green,
Fables dwell, unseen, serene,
Each petal holds a tale to spin,
In nature's realm, where dreams begin.

The brook murmurs of days gone by,
While breezes hum a lullaby,
The roots entwine in age-old lore,
Each whisper tells of love before.

Beneath the sky, in golden light,
Creatures gather in pure delight,
Their stories woven, rich and bold,
In Nature's hands, a treasure unfolds.

The winds that weave through boughs so high,
Carry fables, like birds that fly,
With every gust, a secret shared,
In nature's heart, all is prepared.

So linger long, and let hearts roam,
In forest depths, you'll find your home,
For every breath, a story sings,
In nature's weave, the magic clings.

Silenced Stories of the Mossy Dell

In the vale where whispers dwell,
Old tales weave their magic spell.
Mossy stones hold secrets tight,
Beneath the stars, in velvet night.

Shadows dance on ancient trees,
Carried softly by the breeze.
Echoes of laughter softly sigh,
In the quiet where dreams lie.

Hidden paths of emerald hue,
Call the wanderers, brave and true.
With every step, a tale unfolds,
In timeless woods, where life beholds.

Moonlit glimmers paint the ground,
In gentle arcs, the stillness found.
Hearts entwined with every breath,
Amongst the trees, defying death.

So listen close, to nature's song,
Where the forgotten still belong.
In the mossy dell, stories weave,
Wrapped in dreams, we clasp, believe.

Flickering Lights Among the Foliage

In the forest, shadows play,
Flickers of light, bright as day.
Twinkling gems on leaves so green,
Whispering secrets, soft and serene.

Luminous trails, they guide the way,
Through tangled roots where fairies sway.
Each glimmer sings of ages past,
In a world where time stands vast.

Beneath the boughs, a soft glow spreads,
Cradling dreams on mossy beds.
Every spark, a hope reborn,
In the twilight, where souls are worn.

Rays of starlight, gentle and shy,
Embrace the leaves as night drifts by.
With every flicker, shadows blend,
In nature's dance, no start, no end.

Come find the light within the dark,
Let its warmth ignite a spark.
For in the woods, so lush and bright,
Flickering lights guide lost hearts' flight.

Dancing Dreams on Sylvan Breezes

In the glade where shadows flow,
Dancing dreams begin to grow.
Sylvan breezes hum a tune,
Underneath the silver moon.

Whispers linger, soft and sweet,
As gentle echoes pulse with heat.
Leaves applauding in the night,
A ballet of stars, pure delight.

Fluttering wings of twilight fair,
Mingle with secrets in the air.
Each tender sigh, a wish taken,
In this realm, none are forsaken.

Through the branches, laughter twirls,
As every heartbeat gently unfurls.
Nature's canvas, vast and bright,
Painted in shades of pure moonlight.

So come and dance this night away,
In dreams where spirit will not sway.
For in this realm of boundless thought,
Dancing dreams can't be caught.

Amidst the Thickets of Wonder

In thickets deep, where magic lies,
Wonder blooms beneath the skies.
Curled up roots, a hidden door,
To realms where tales wait to explore.

Branches twist in playful cheer,
As laughter dances, bright and clear.
Every leaf a story tells,
In the heart of mossy dells.

Ferns unfurl, with secrets bold,
Guardians of stories yet untold.
Beneath the canopy's embrace,
Adventures weave in every space.

Softly nestled, creatures pause,
To listen close to nature's laws.
With every rustle, magic stirs,
In thickets rich with life's soft purrs.

So venture forth, let wonder reign,
In the thickets, let joy unstain.
For in this world, enchantment brews,
A journey waits for those who choose.

The Eldritch Choir of Leaves

In twilight's hush, the whispers rise,
As branches sing to dusky skies.
Each leaf a note in nature's song,
An ancient chorus, deep and strong.

They rustle tales of days long lost,
Of magic found at midnight's cost.
In shadows, secrets swirl and twine,
Where dreams awaken, bright and divine.

Beneath the boughs of oak and pine,
The echoes weave through time like twine.
A harmony of softest breath,
That lingers long, defying death.

Their voices dance on evening air,
A tapestry both bold and rare.
Each rustle shared between the trees,
An eldritch hymn on twilight's breeze.

Now silence falls, the night is near,
Yet in the heart, the music clear.
For those who listen, hearts aglow,
The choir sings, in leaves that grow.

Beneath the Silver-Barked Trees

Underneath the silver bark,
Where whispers dwell and shadows hark,
The forest holds its secrets tight,
Bathed in the soft, ethereal light.

With every step, a story calls,
Where ancient magic always falls.
The roots entwined like tales of old,
In every cell, a truth untold.

The air imbibes a mystic sigh,
As gentle breezes waltz and fly.
Each silver thread in twilight spun,
A haven found where dreams begun.

Down winding paths where echoes play,
The spirits of the night delay.
To share their wisdom, hide away,
Within the trees, where shadows sway.

So linger here, let worries cease,
Beneath the boughs, discover peace.
With eyes alight and hearts set free,
Within this realm, just you and me.

Starlit Secrets of the Glade

In a glade where starlight falls,
The nightingale serenely calls.
With shimmering shards of silver light,
The secrets bloom, softly at night.

Wildflowers awaken, hues aglow,
Their petals whisper things we know.
Each star above a watchful eye,
That glimmers sweetly, nigh or nigh.

The trees embrace the cosmic lore,
As branches sway and spirits soar.
A magic palpable and near,
Where wishes whispered ignite cheer.

As shadows dance on velvet ground,
A world anew in silence found.
With hearts aligned to nature's beat,
The glade unfolds, both wild and sweet.

So gather near the glowing streams,
And share in all the starlit dreams.
For in this place, our spirits mend,
The secrets shared will never end.

Reflections of the Enchanted Wilds

In wilds alive with emerald grace,
Each creature finds its rightful place.
A mirror of the heart's desire,
Where nature thrives and dreams conspire.

The brook that babbles tales of yore,
Invites the weary, seek to explore.
With laughter mingling in the air,
The wilds invite, with gentle care.

An owl calls out, a sentinel,
While shadows weave their potent spell.
The moonlight drapes the world in dreams,
As every glance reflects and gleams.

The night unfolds, a velvet sheet,
Each step we take, a fable sweet.
In every echo of the wild,
We find our love, as nature's child.

So roam these lands with heart ablaze,
And let your spirit join the praise.
For in the wilds, forever free,
We find ourselves, eternally.

Legends in the Embrace of Flora

In the glen where shadows dance,
Whispers weave, a mystic trance.
Petals soft and colors bright,
Guard old tales in morning light.

From the boughs, a voice calls clear,
Echoes of the ones held dear.
Marvels bloom where dreams entwine,
In the heart of verdant vine.

Beneath the arch of emerald leaves,
Nature's breath, the spirit weaves.
Fables woven tight with grace,
In the earth's warm, soft embrace.

Amidst the roots, old stories creep,
In their cradle, secrets sleep.
Every petal, twig, and thorn,
Holds a tale of magic born.

Through the trees, the moonlight spills,
Over silent, gentle hills.
Legends rise and softly sink,
In every fragrant bloom, we think.

Secrets Cradled in Gnarled Roots

In the dark where shadows hide,
Gnarled roots twist, a secret guide.
Softly tangled, tales unfold,
In the silence, wisps of old.

Beneath the earth, a story sown,
In whispers low, the past has grown.
Branches arch like ancient lore,
Guarding truths forevermore.

Footfalls echo through the night,
As the stars claim their height.
Smoky dreams in quiet thrum,
Buried deep, the secrets hum.

Each flicker of the fire's glow,
Reveals the paths where few dare go.
In the hush, a promise made,
By the roots, those bonds won't fade.

Hideaways in nature's heart,
Treasure troves where shadows part.
Every curl, each twist and bend,
Whispers softly, 'We transcend.'

The Enchanted Path of Ancient Footsteps

Through the woods, where legends sleep,
Footsteps echo, secrets keep.
Ancient stones, all mossy green,
Mark the paths where dreams have been.

With each step, the air turns rare,
Magic thrums in the twilight air.
Moonlit glades where fabled beings,
Softly tread with gentle leanings.

Whispers linger on the breeze,
Songs of leaves on slumbering trees.
Cloaked in night, the spirits roam,
Guiding souls to find their home.

Dances held in shadowed glen,
Woven threads of now and then.
Every stone, a tale to tell,
Each turn leads to where dreams dwell.

In echoes past, the heart will find,
A timeless quest, lovingly kind.
Take the path, let wonders grow,
On this journey, let love flow.

Reveries in the Whispering Winds

When the winds weave their gentle song,
Hearts awake, where dreams belong.
Echoes dance upon the air,
Soft caresses, sweet and rare.

Through the meadows, sunlight streams,
Carrying with it cherished dreams.
Leaves flutter, secrets shared,
In the whispers, love is bared.

Voices calling through the night,
Guiding souls towards the light.
Embers glow, and shadows play,
In the whispers, night turns day.

As the evening drapes its shawl,
Stars awaken, one and all.
With each breeze, a promise flows,
In the stillness, magic grows.

Let the winds by heart embrace,
In their dance, we find our place.
Through the night and into dawn,
In reveries, our hopes are drawn.

The Elven Lorekeeper's Secrets

In shadows deep where whispers dwell,
The lorekeeper guards tales to tell.
With ancient scrolls and ink so rare,
He spins the magic heavy in air.

Beneath the moon's soft, silvery glow,
He weaves the strands of time's flow.
A flicker of stars in his wise eyes,
Unlocking truths beneath the skies.

Each secret bound in woven dreams,
With threads of fate that gently gleam.
The echoes of ages softly sing,
As knowledge flows from the elder's wing.

His fingers dance on parchment pale,
Revealing paths through misty veil.
A lorekeeper of wondrous might,
In twilight's grasp, he guards the light.

Through ages past and futures bright,
His heart beats strong with ancient rite.
For every tale cast in the night,
Holds hidden magic, pure delight.

Threads of Fantasy in Twilight

In twilight hues where day meets night,
Dreams awaken, taking flight.
Threads of fantasy gently weave,
A tapestry of what we believe.

With every star that graces skies,
A spark of wonder softly lies.
In whispered tales of old, retold,
New worlds beneath the dusk unfold.

Shadows dance with ghosts of yore,
As magic breathes through every door.
The flutter of wings, the rhythm of hearts,
In this realm, reality departs.

Time bends softly, a fluid stream,
Where wishes linger in a dream.
The horizon blurs, the colors blend,
In twilight's grasp, all limits end.

With every sigh, a story spins,
In the balance where magic begins.
Threads of fate entwine with glee,
In twilight's arms, we soar, we're free.

Echoes of a Forgotten Glade

In a glade where silence reigns,
Whispers linger through the lanes.
Echoes dance on the gentle breeze,
Carrying secrets from ancient trees.

Sunlight dapples through the leaves,
As gentle shadows weave their eves.
Memories pulse in the mossy ground,
In every corner, the past is found.

Lost in a world of emerald hue,
The glade holds legends, old yet new.
A serene chorus sings through the air,
Of dreams long faded, once laid bare.

With every rustle, the stories call,
Tales of triumph, and those who fall.
Time pauses there, a sacred space,
In the glade's embrace, we find our place.

Beneath the boughs where echoes dwell,
In chambers deep, the spirits swell.
With every heartbeat, the glade remains,
A haven of wonder, a place unexplained.

Beneath the Shimmering Bough

Beneath the boughs where fairies play,
The world transforms at close of day.
With glimmers bright and laughter sweet,
They weave enchantments with nimble feet.

In moonlit fields of silver bright,
Magic stirs in the cool twilight.
Breezes carry a lilting song,
As secrets beckon to wanderers long.

The air is thick with fragrant blooms,
Where twilight hushes the evening's glooms.
Stars awaken, painting the skies,
Illuminating dreams where wonder lies.

In the flicker of wings, adventures rise,
Stories twinkling in twinkling eyes.
A safe haven in nature's art,
Where each whisper entrances the heart.

So linger long 'neath the shimmering bough,
Embrace the magic, forget your vow.
For in this realm of pure delight,
The heart finds freedom in the night.

The Lament of the Enchanted Boughs

In twilight's hush, the boughs do sigh,
With whispers soft as shadows fly.
The moonlight weaves through emerald leaves,
Where ancient magic hardly grieves.

A tale of love, of loss, and time,
Each branch a story, each root a rhyme.
They bend and sway in the gentle breeze,
Speaking secrets to wandering trees.

When starlit nights bewitch the ground,
Echoes of laughter, no longer found.
The forest weeps for those long gone,
Their echoes linger, a haunting song.

Through tangled paths, where spirits roam,
Even the lost can find a home.
For every tear that the boughs have shed,
A thousand more love stories are fed.

In the heart of woods, where dreams conspire,
Hope blends with heartache, a flickering fire.
The enchanted boughs, in their quiet despair,
Stand sentinel over what once was fair.

Chronicles of the Spirit-Drenched Path

Upon the path where shadows dwell,
History weaves its timeless spell.
With every step, the spirits speak,
In whispers soft, they rise and peak.

Moss-covered stones tell tales of old,
A journey wrapped in threads of gold.
Through every bend, a memory lies,
Beneath the fabric of starlit skies.

Each rustling leaf, a sigh of fate,
A symphony of hearts that wait.
They beckon forth with promises bright,
Guiding lost souls toward the light.

While twilight shadows dance and twine,
The path reveals its secret line.
Here courage blooms in the shrouded night,
Where dreams ignite with newfound light.

So tread with care on this sacred way,
For echoes linger and wish to stay.
Embrace the magic; let it flow,
In the spirit-drenched path, let your heart grow.

The Dance of Faeries at Dusk

As twilight drapes the emerald glen,
The faeries twirl where they have been.
On petals soft, their laughter blends,
With whispers low that night descends.

With gossamer wings in moonlit grace,
They chase the stars in a boundless space.
Beneath the trees, where secrets lie,
They spin their dreams, as shadows sigh.

In circles wide, they weave and sway,
A spell that keeps the dark at bay.
With every flicker of their light,
They paint the world in shades of night.

The breeze, it carries their sweet song,
A melody where hearts belong.
With laughter bright and hearts so free,
The faeries dance in harmony.

As dawn approaches, softly sighs,
They bid farewell beneath the skies.
Yet in the dew, their magic stays,
To greet the world in morning's rays.

Chronicles of Sylvan Shadows

In whispers deep, the forest breathes,
An ancient tale in rustling leaves.
Beneath the boughs where shadows creep,
The secrets of the woods they keep.

Through tangled roots and winding trails,
Echo the stories of olden tales.
In every nook, a memory stirs,
Of knights and quests, and silent furs.

With every step, the echoes chime,
A journey forged in the sands of time.
From twilight's grasp to morning's light,
The chronicles weave through day and night.

In glades where ancient spirits roam,
Each tale finds heart, each heart finds home.
Together bound, in woods they dwell,
The whispers weave their timeless spell.

So let the wanderers tread with care,
For shadows cling, and truths lay bare.
In sylvan realms, where legends thrive,
The past and present come alive.

Where Legends Dwell in Silence

In hollows deep, where shadows blend,
The echoes of old legends send.
A breeze that carries whispered lore,
In silence speaks of yore once more.

Each stone and stream, a fable tells,
Of heroes bold and magic spells.
Beneath the stars, where dreams converge,
The heart of time begins to surge.

In quiet groves where spirits rest,
The past entwines with every quest.
Here, quietude wraps the soul,
While memory weaves its gentle scroll.

With each soft rustle of the leaves,
The tales of valor gently breathe.
In the stillness, wisdom grows,
As ancient truth in silence flows.

So linger long where legends throng,
In the sacred hush where they belong.
For in the silence, all is clear,
The magic lives when we draw near.

Mystical Paths Through the Woodland

Through tangled paths of emerald green,
Mysterious wonders, yet unseen.
The woodland calls with a siren's tune,
As whims of fate are spun by moon.

In dappled light, enchanted sights,
Awaken dreams on starry nights.
Where every step could stir the air,
And magic lingers everywhere.

With every turn, a tale unfolds,
Of creatures fierce and hearts of gold.
In gentle glades where fairies play,
The woodland magic invites us to stay.

Through whispers of the ancient trees,
The spirits dance upon the breeze.
Guiding those who seek to roam,
To find the magic they can call home.

So wander forth with open hearts,
And let the woodland weave its arts.
For in its paths, we find our way,
To mystical realms where dreams hold sway.

Guardians of the Ethereal Realm

In shadows deep, where starlight gleams,
The guardians weave celestial dreams.
With whispered spells and ancient lore,
They guard the gates forevermore.

Upon the wind, their voices soar,
Echoing through the mystic door.
With eyes like stars, they glimpse the truth,
In realms where time preserves its youth.

Through twilight paths, the fae do dance,
In moonlit glades, they weave romance.
Each flicker bright, a tale untold,
Of worlds where magic sings bold.

When shadows fall and silence reigns,
The guardians hum their gentle strains.
A pact with night, forever tight,
To keep the balance 'twixt dark and light.

So heed the call of dusky skies,
For in the dreams, the magic lies.
And in the depths of night's embrace,
The guardians hold a sacred space.

Tales Whispered by the Moonlight

Upon the hill, the old tales rise,
Beneath the moon's enchanted guise.
Each silver beam, a story spun,
Of love and loss, of battles won.

The whispering winds carry the lore,
From ancient times to future's shore.
With every breath, the night reveals,
The secrets time so gently wields.

In quiet glades where shadows play,
The spirits dance the night away.
And in their sway, a truth alights,
That dreams are born on starry nights.

Each foxglove bloom and moonlit stream,
Holds echoes of a lingering dream.
With every sigh, the night enfolds,
The whispers of the heart, so bold.

So gather 'round, as tales unfold,
With every word, a world retold.
In moonlight's glow, let spirits soar,
For tales of old forevermore.

The Song of the Emerald Canopy

In forests deep, where shadows play,
Emerald leaves sway night and day.
With rustling whispers and gentle sighs,
The canopies hold the earth's wise cries.

Each branch a story, each root a song,
Of ancient tales where we belong.
In twilight's hush, the whispers weave,
A harmony that we believe.

The creatures small, the spirits bright,
Join in the dance beneath the light.
With every note, the woodlands hum,
In songs of life, they bravely come.

Through vibrant blooms and winding trails,
The essence of the forest sails.
A symphony of nature's grace,
In every heartbeat, time we trace.

So linger here, in beauty's throng,
Embrace the world, where you belong.
For in this grove, the heart takes flight,
In the emerald canopy's endless night.

Dreaming in the Faerie Circle

In faerie circles, dreams take flight,
With petals soft and gleaming light.
They dance in rings where magic flows,
And weave the dreams that nature knows.

With laughter sweet, they call the night,
In twinkling stars, pure delight.
A world of whispers, secrets deep,
Where time stands still and shadows leap.

Each glimmering dewdrop holds a tale,
Of secret paths and gentle trails.
In every flicker, magic sings,
Of moonlit nights and fairy wings.

When children dream and hearts align,
In softly spun, enchanting twine.
The fae invite with gentle grace,
To join the dance in this sacred space.

So close your eyes and drift afar,
To realms of light, where wishes are.
In faerie circles, love abounds,
As dreams awaken, joy resounds.

Epiphanies in the Charmed Woods

In a grove where whispers weave,
Moonlight dances on the leaves.
Secrets hidden from our sight,
Nature's magic blooms at night.

A soft glow from the heart of trees,
Carried gently on the breeze.
Every shadow tells a tale,
In this wood where dreams set sail.

Footsteps light as a feather's fall,
Ancient echoes beckon all.
Fingers brush the bark so wise,
Awakening the stars in skies.

With each breath, a revelation,
Cradled in the forest's foundation.
Wisdom flows in the twilight air,
Inviting souls to linger there.

Transcend the world of mere illusion,
Find the heart in spirit's fusion.
In the embrace of nature's grace,
We discover our rightful place.

The Unseen Threads of Nature's Tapestry

Weaving softly, day by day,
Nature spins a grand ballet.
Invisible threads connect us all,
In every rise and every fall.

The brook sings songs of ancient lore,
And the mountains echo more.
A tapestry of life unfurls,
Binding hearts in hidden swirls.

Dew-kissed petals glisten bright,
Catching whispers of the night.
In the silence, wisdom flows,
With every thread, the spirit grows.

The dance of leaves, a timeless art,
Each movement felt within the heart.
Nature's fibers intricately spun,
Embrace the magic—everyone.

So look around, and you will see,
The unseen bonds of earth and tree.
In nature's weave, we find our way,
A united song at the break of day.

The Glimmering Heart of Faerytide

In twilight's glow, the fairies play,
Beneath the stars where wishes sway.
Their laughter rings like silver chimes,
Echoing through the ancient pines.

A glimmering heart in the forest deep,
In shadows where secrets choose to sleep.
Dancing lights in radiant flight,
Guide the lost through the veil of night.

Flowers bloom with vibrant grace,
Imbued with magic, full of grace.
Tender moments held so dear,
The faerytide draws us near.

With every flutter, dreams ignite,
In realms where time takes gentle flight.
Embraced within this sacred space,
We find ourselves through nature's face.

So let the faeries take your hand,
And lead you to the wonderland.
Where glimmering hearts forever gleam,
And magic weaves the sweetest dream.

Murmurs of the Eldest Trees

In ancient woods where silence breathes,
Reside the murmurs of the trees.
Their gnarled roots hold stories old,
Whispering secrets yet untold.

With branches strong, they kiss the sky,
Guardians of time as seasons fly.
Each rustling leaf recalls a song,
A harmony where we belong.

Life cascades in green and gold,
As echoes ring of tales retold.
In every ring, a year preserved,
Nature's wisdom, richly conserved.

Beneath their shade, the world feels bright,
In their embrace, all wrongs feel right.
They share the dreams of earth and air,
A timeless bond beyond compare.

So pause awhile under their gaze,
And listen close to ancient ways.
The eldest trees, with steady grace,
Invite us to their sacred space.

Legends of the Emerald Ring

In ancient woods where shadows weave,
A tale of magic we believe.
The emerald ring, a gem so bright,
Holds secrets whispered in the night.

Fairies dance in twilight's glow,
Their laughter echoes soft and low.
Guardians of the ring they seek,
With glowing eyes and voices meek.

In circles drawn with emerald hue,
The chosen gather, brave and true.
They speak of dreams both old and new,
Of quests that only few pursue.

Yet danger lurks within the glade,
A curse that never seems to fade.
For those who seek the ring's great power,
Must brave the storm, the thunder shower.

But hope abounds within the green,
For friendship blooms where few have seen.
Together, hand in hand, they'll stand,
With hearts united, bold and grand.

The Mystical Veil of Night

Beneath the stars, where shadows play,
A veil descends, both dark and gray.
It weaves a world of dreams untold,
Where mysteries in silence unfold.

The moonlight dances on the stream,
While nightingale sings a soothing theme.
Secrets fester in dusky air,
Whispers twine, a haunting flare.

A cloak of night, both soft and tight,
Hides ancient wonders out of sight.
With every rustle, stories sigh,
As silence breathes a gentle lie.

Yet brave the hearts who roam the night,
With lanterns lit, their spirits bright.
They seek the truth that darkness keeps,
To waken dreams from slumbered sleeps.

Through enchanted woods, they make their way,
Where shadows flicker, dance, and sway.
In the depths of night, hope remains,
A guiding star that never wanes.

Celestial Threads of the Forest

In tangled boughs where starlight weaves,
The forest hums, the daylight leaves.
Each branch a thread, so finely spun,
Connecting all beneath the sun.

The whispers of the ancient trees,
Tell stories carried on the breeze.
Their roots stretch far, in soil deep,
Guarding secrets they long to keep.

Celestial paths crisscross above,
A dance of light, a song of love.
With every rustle, life awakes,
A tapestry that fate creates.

The creatures small, the ones unseen,
Thread through the woods, both fierce and keen.
A woven fate, a magic rare,
In leafy spaces, everywhere.

With open hearts, we wander here,
Each step we take draws us near.
To understand the threads that bind,
The stories etched in nature's mind.

Fables from the Faerie Ring

Round and round the faeries twirl,
In every heart, a magic whirl.
They weave their tales in moonlit mist,
Of whispered dreams that can't be missed.

In circles spun with laughter light,
They gather 'neath the stars so bright.
With every tale, a spark ignites,
As joy and wonder claim the night.

Their fables hold a truth profound,
In every story, wisdom found.
Lessons learned from ancient times,
In rhythm sweet as nursery rhymes.

Yet tread with care on faerie ground,
For mischief lurks where dreams abound.
A promise made, a fate entwined,
Can lead the heart where love is blind.

So sit awhile and listen dear,
To fables whispered, soft and clear.
With open hearts, let magic sing,
In every tale, a faerie's ring.

Reflections of the Silvan Spirits

In the glade where whispers dwell,
Silvan spirits weave their spell.
With each breeze, a story sings,
Of ancient trees and quiet things.

Moonbeams dance on silver streams,
Weaving through our twilight dreams.
Echoes of the past arise,
Underneath the starlit skies.

In shadows deep, they find their dance,
Call of magic, a fleeting glance.
With gentle sighs, the forest breathes,
As twilight wraps and softly weaves.

Where the nightingale takes flight,
Glowing softly, our hearts ignite.
Each rustle speaks of secrets old,
In silver leaves their tales unfold.

Through the mist, their voices twine,
In every flicker, a glimmered sign.
The silvan spirits, ever near,
Guard the echoes we hold dear.

Dance of Shadows and Starlight

Underneath the crescent glow,
Shadows dance, quiet and slow.
Stars above in silence gleam,
Weaving softly like a dream.

In the hush of midnight air,
Whispers of the heart laid bare.
Each flicker tells a tale anew,
Of wishes old and visions true.

Amidst the trees, they twist and weave,
Taking form in moonlit eves.
Echoing the light's embrace,
In their rhythm, we find grace.

With every step, the night exhales,
Binding us with unseen trails.
In this waltz of dusk and dew,
Shadows merge, as dreams come true.

In the space where moments twine,
Magic flows in every line.
Holding tight to fate's strange weave,
We dance on, we dare believe.

The Glistening Path of Fables

Along the glistening, winding way,
Fables bloom in bright array.
With each step upon the leaves,
We gather tales like summer eves.

Beneath the boughs, a secret hum,
Echoes soft of tales long spun.
In whispers soft, the past concedes,
As every heart learns, every heart needs.

Dancing light through branches plays,
Illuminating hidden bays.
Eager souls, in wonder born,
Chase the dreams of stories worn.

Among the roots, adventures stir,
In every bark, a gentle blur.
With every glance, a thrill unfolds,
In the language of the bold.

Footprints mark the knowing ground,
Where echoes of our hearts resound.
In every turn, a truth awaits,
In fable's arms, we find our fates.

Secrets Beneath Mossy Cover

Underneath the mossy shroud,
Whispers linger, soft and loud.
Secrets held in nature's grasp,
Waiting gently to unmask.

In the twilight, shadows blend,
Nature's tales begin to bend.
Covered roots and ancient stones,
Guard the dreams of silent moans.

With each footstep on the earth,
We unlock the weight of worth.
In every creak of swaying wood,
Lie the stories, misunderstood.

Beneath the green, life hums and sways,
In whispers soft, it sings our praise.
The air is thick with twilight's breath,
In the hidden, we find depth.

Trust the silence, let it seep,
In the places shadows keep.
For underneath this ancient cover,
Lies a heart that beats like thunder.

Chants of the Verdant Spirits

In the whispers of the leaves, they sing,
Ethereal echoes of the ancient spring.
Softly woven through the emerald sighs,
Nature's melody beneath the vast skies.

Children of the earth, they dance in the breeze,
Spirits of the forest, boundless as the seas.
With every rustle, tales of yore unfurl,
Their harmony resounds in a vibrant whirl.

In the shade of oaks, they weave their delight,
Casting shadows that twinkle in the night.
Flickers of laughter, amidst the glens,
A secret language where the magic begins.

Embrace the hush as they beckon you near,
In their gentle songs, no reason to fear.
Through dappled sunlight, their legacy flows,
Awakening wonders where the wildflower grows.

So listen closely, to the verdant call,
For within each tone, lies the heart of it all.
A symphony sung by the wise and the free,
In the realms of the green, forever shall be.

The Language of Forgotten Blossoms

Beneath the soil where the shadows meet,
Lie whispers of petals, soft, bittersweet.
Each bud a story, waiting to bloom,
In silence, they shelter, the secrets of gloom.

Winds carry murmurs from places unseen,
Where time weaves its fabric, with threads of green.
Forgotten dreams dance on the tip of a stem,
Echoes of laughter, like a delicate hymn.

Petals unfurl in the gentle sun's light,
Breathing life into tales, shadowed from sight.
In colors forgotten, their voices entwine,
Each hue a memory, pure and divine.

Lost in the garden where time stands still,
The blossoms awaken, as hearts start to fill.
With every new season, they weave and they spin,
A tapestry rich, where life can begin.

So gather the petals, recall what they say,
For in their soft murmurs, magic finds way.
In the hush of the twilight, let their tales soar,
Unlocking the portals to beauty once more.

Enigmas of the Twilight Thicket

Where shadows dance and the twilight ignites,
Lies a thicket of secrets under the night.
Bristling with mysteries, whispers take flight,
In the hush of the woods, it holds the moonlight.

Deep in the thicket, the shadows conspire,
Foxes and owls, in council, desire.
The rustle of branches, a soft, tender plea,
Voices of nightfall, wild and carefree.

A lantern of stars weaves stories sublime,
Illuminating pathways through echoes of time.
With each step you take, the universe bends,
In the tapestry woven, where magic transcends.

The flutter of wings, a spark in the dark,
Calls forth the spirits as the night leaves its mark.
In the twilight thicket, enchantments await,
Infinite wonders where dreams resonate.

So wander these woods where the enigma stays,
In every corner, a labyrinth plays.
Breathe deep the magic that lingers and stirs,
For the twilight's embrace forever endures.

Phantoms in the Dappled Shade

In the quiet corners where whispers abide,
Phantoms of memories linger and bide.
Dappled shade softens the edges of time,
Ghostly apparitions in moments sublime.

Sunlight cascades through leaves overhead,
Illuminating paths where the dreamers once tread.
Their laughter still echoes in the rustling air,
Unseen yet felt, a presence laid bare.

Amongst the tall grasses, they twirl and delight,
Figures of twilight, vanishing from sight.
In their gentle dance, the past overlaps,
A tapestry woven from forgotten maps.

With each passing breeze, their stories unfurl,
In the dappled shade, where mysteries swirl.
Embrace the enchantment that whispers your name,
For the phantoms you seek are never the same.

So linger awhile, in this twilight's embrace,
Feel the warmth of a long-lost place.
In the heart of the wood, let your spirit be free,
Among phantoms of shade, find your reverie.

The Secrets of the Starlit Ring

In whispers soft, the night does speak,
A silvered light, the shadows seek.
Among the stars, a tale is spun,
Of magic bright, and dreams begun.

The velvet sky, a canvas wide,
Where secrets hide, and wishes bide.
Each twinkling gem a wish fulfilled,
In the heart of night, love is distilled.

The moonlit path, a guide so true,
In silent woods where wonders grew.
Beneath the arch, the starlit ring,
The echo of an ancient fling.

A tapestry of fate entwined,
Where hearts align and souls are mined.
With every pulse, a rhythm beats,
The universe, our dance completes.

Through cosmic realms, the dreamers soar,
To find the keys to mystery's door.
With starlit grace, we spin and twirl,
In the night's embrace, our hearts unfurl.

Lullabies of the Woodland Spirits

In twilight's hush, the forest hums,
Where gentle winds and magic drums.
The spirits sing in soft refrain,
With lullabies that ease the pain.

Beneath the boughs, where shadows creep,
The woodland whispers secrets deep.
Their melodies, like rivers flow,
In dreamy notes, they weave and glow.

A dance of leaves, they swirl and play,
As stars emerge and chase the day.
Each fleeting sound, a story shared,
Of ancient tales, long lost, yet bared.

The moonlight spills on glen and brook,
Enchanting sights, in every nook.
The spirits gather, hearts entwined,
In lullabies, a peace we find.

And as the night draws ever near,
The whispers calm, dissolve our fear.
In dream-woven realms, we gently fall,
Cradled by the woodland's call.

The Gathering Under the Ancient Oak

Beneath the branches, wisdom stands,
The ancient oak, with gnarled hands.
In shadows deep, the friends convene,
A gathering where hearts are seen.

With laughter sweet, the tales unfold,
Of quests and dreams, of heroes bold.
In whispered tones, the night expands,
As starlit skies embrace our plans.

A rustic feast, laid out with care,
The bonds of friendship linger there.
In every bite, the magic swells,
As stories weave their timeless spells.

The fire crackles, embers dance,
In flickering light, we steal a glance.
A heartbeat shared, a fleeting pause,
In unity, we find our cause.

The oak stands watch, its roots run deep,
In ancient ground, the dreams we keep.
With whispered charms, the night draws near,
Together strong, we banish fear.

Enchantment in a Silvered Glade

In glades aglow with silver light,
Where shadows play and spirits ignite.
The air is thick with magic's breath,
A dance of life, defying death.

The flowers bloom like stars on earth,
Each petal holds a whispered birth.
The brook hums tunes of ages past,
In every ripple, spells are cast.

As twilight drapes its cloak so fine,
The world transforms, and all align.
With every star that graces night,
We gather 'round in shared delight.

The trees sway gently, soft and low,
Their branches weave a lace of glow.
Each sigh of wind, a story spins,
In this silver glade, the magic begins.

So come and dance, let spirits soar,
In enchanted realms, we'll seek for more.
With hearts aflame and laughter bright,
In silvered glades, we find our light.

Arcane Rituals in Twilight

In the hush of the waning light,
Whispers weave through the air,
Echoes of a forgotten rite,
Gathered souls that dare.

Candles flicker, shadows dance,
Glimmers of ancient lore,
Starlit skies that seem to prance,
Invoke what lies in store.

Runes are etched in the earth,
Charged with power yet unseen,
Beneath the moon, a rebirth,
Mysteries wrapped in green.

Time eludes in this embrace,
Moments stretch and then collide,
Every heart finds its own pace,
Magic flows like a tide.

As the final words take flight,
Beneath a veil of night's caress,
The arcane secrets set alight,
In twilight's stillness, bless.

The Grove's Hidden Chronicles

Deep within the emerald hold,
Lies a tale of yore,
In whispers soft, the trees unfold,
Their secrets to explore.

Mossy stones and twisted roots,
Guard the legends past,
Tales of fairies, lost pursuits,
In shadows cast so vast.

A brook sings songs of ages lost,
Reflecting dreams anew,
Every ripple bears the cost,
Of magic's hidden view.

Beneath the boughs of ancient oaks,
The spirits softly sigh,
Each groan a memory evokes,
Underneath the vast sky.

When twilight drapes its cloak of night,
The grove begins to breathe,
A world of wonders, pure delight,
In branches, dreams we weave.

Beneath the Canopy of Dreams

In slumber's grasp, where dreams reside,
A canvas weaves its art,
Beneath the stars, where hopes abide,
And whispering thoughts depart.

Clouds float gently, soft as sighs,
Beneath the moon's embrace,
A world that shimmers, never dies,
A tranquil, hidden place.

Each moment drapes in silver hue,
Carried on a breeze,
A lullaby of wishes true,
Entwined like gentle trees.

The night conceals what dawn will find,
A treasure yet to bloom,
In silence, secrets intertwine,
Embracing evening's gloom.

Awake, the past begins to fade,
Yet echoes softly call,
Beneath the dreams that softly laid,
A magic over all.

Enchantment at Dusk's Threshold

As daylight bids its fond farewell,
A charm ignites within the dusk,
Where embers of the twilight swell,
In shadows, secrets husk.

The air is thick with silent spells,
Serenading the farewell light,
In every corner, magic dwells,
Transforming day to night.

Glimmers twine in the crisp air,
A tapestry of dreams unfold,
In the ancient, lingering glare,
New stories yet untold.

Every fading hue holds sway,
In reverence to the unseen,
Mirthful ghosts of yesterday,
Dance within the evergreen.

With the stars, enchantments bloom,
In whispers soft, they soar,
Dusk, the softest cradle's loom,
Creating evermore.

The Dance of the Ancient Spirits

In the grove where shadows play,
Whispers hum of yesterday,
Leaves twirl soft with every breath,
Echoes stir from silent death.

Glowing orbs in moonlit sway,
Guide the spirits through their ballet,
Threads of time entwine and weave,
Magic stirs for those who believe.

Footfalls light on velvet ground,
Nature's song, a haunting sound,
Each heartbeat matched to the skies,
Where the dance of wisdom lies.

Beneath the arch of ancient trees,
Rustling leaves whispering with ease,
Ancient eyes now glimmer bright,
Guiding souls through the quiet night.

With every turn, the night's embrace,
The spirits twirl in their sacred space,
To the rhythm of the timeless breeze,
In the dance of life, hearts find ease.

Silhouettes Under the Starlit Canopy

Silhouettes beneath the glow,
Whispers soft, like falling snow,
Starlit dreams twist high above,
In the night, we find our love.

Branches reach like fingers fair,
Caressing hearts in cool night air,
With every breath, the moonlight streams,
Crafting visions, lacing dreams.

In the dark, our stories blend,
Secret tales that never end,
Constellations spin and sway,
As we dance the night away.

Glimmers bright spark hope anew,
Each shared glance, a promise true,
Underneath the heavens' sway,
Love ignites where shadows play.

As dawn's first light begins to glow,
Memories of starlit show,
Fading echoes of our night,
Promising tomorrow's light.

Echoes of Forgotten Lore

In the woods where whispers dwell,
Echoes of old stories tell,
Voices carried by the breeze,
Secrets hidden in the trees.

Ancient runes on stones well worn,
Speak of magic, lost and torn,
Fables of the brave and wise,
Caught in time, where mystery lies.

Listen close, the murmurs call,
From the shadows, rise and fall,
Tales of kings and lost desires,
Woven near the flickering fires.

In the silence, voices weave,
Through the night, they beg to leave,
Cloaked in mist, they draw us near,
Echoes rich with joy and fear.

Gather 'round as stories flow,
With every word, our hearts do grow,
Rooted deep in ancient lore,
Together, we will seek for more.

The Elfin Reverie

In the glade where fairies dream,
Moonlit glimmers softly beam,
Magic flows like whispers sweet,
Underneath their dancing feet.

Gentle laughter fills the air,
Elfin songs, a song to share,
Every note a silver thread,
Weaving magic where we tread.

Through the flowers, sunlight streams,
Each petal holds enchanting dreams,
Elves and whispers twine as one,
In the light of setting sun.

With a twirl and playful glance,
Join their ever-spinning dance,
Worlds align in joyous flight,
Where the day melts into night.

As the stars begin to wink,
In a world where moments sink,
Elfin glooms and gleams unite,
In this reverie of light.

Whispers of Enchanted Realms

In glades where shadows softly play,
The whispers of the night will sway,
A dance of light in silver streams,
Where every heart holds secret dreams.

Among the ferns and ancient trees,
The gentle sighing of the breeze,
Carries stories from the past,
In every moment, fleeting, vast.

With echoes of a timeless song,
The magic calls, where souls belong,
And in the dusk, the magic's quilt,
In dreams of wonder, softly built.

The stars above, a jeweled sea,
Guide weary hearts to set them free,
Where golden paths of hope entwine,
And every wish begins to shine.

So linger here, the twilight's glow,
Where all the hidden secrets flow,
In whispered tones, the world unfurls,
In whispers of enchanted worlds.

Secrets Beneath the Canopy

Beneath the weave of leafy lace,
The mysteries of time embrace,
A rustle here, a flash of wing,
The forest's breath begins to sing.

In shadows deep, where silence weaves,
And sunlight spills like golden leaves,
The stories linger, age-old spells,
In every nook, where magic dwells.

Soft murmurs of the woodland thrive,
With whispers that keep dreams alive,
A tapestry of sight and sound,
Where secrets of the earth abound.

The tendrils of the roots entwined,
Hold tales that wander, almost blind,
With every step, a spark ignites,
In secrets found, in hidden lights.

So tread with care, where wonders lie,
And listen as the branches sigh,
For in the quiet, truth is spun,
In secrets beneath the canopy.

Tales from the Glimmering Grove

In twilight's hush, the grove awakes,
With glowing lights and silver flakes,
Each step unveils a whispered tale,
Where dreams and magic never pale.

The moonlit dance of fairy wings,
In shimmering air, the starlight sings,
Each petal shines, a story bright,
In every drop of gleaming light.

The ancient oaks, with voices low,
Share secrets of the long ago,
And lanterns hung on every bough,
Illuminate the here and now.

With every breeze, the echoes flow,
Of whispered hopes that softly glow,
In laughter shared 'neath boughs that sway,
The glimmering grove keeps dreams at bay.

So wander through this sacred space,
And find the magic that you trace,
For tales of wonder softly weave,
In tales from grove where hearts believe.

Nightshade Dreams in the Moonlight

In moonlit glades where night takes flight,
The dreams of shadow bask in light,
With whispers cloaked in silken dark,
Nightshade blooms, a tender spark.

The velvet sky wraps all in hush,
As fireflies paint the night with brush,
Of gentle hopes and silver beams,
In nightshade dreams, the heart redeems.

The whispered lore of stars above,
With every glance, the heart will love,
And wrapped in stillness, visions gleam,
In darkened woods, we share our dream.

When shadows play and secrets sway,
The night unfolds in rich array,
Through tangled paths of stillness deep,
Where nightshade dreams in moonlight seep.

So linger close, let thoughts take flight,
In dreams that rise within the night,
For in each breath, enchantments weave,
In nightshade dreams, we dare believe.

The Timeless Oath of the Forest

In shadows deep where secrets dwell,
The trees entwine, their tales to tell.
A vow they keep, in silent grace,
The timeless oath of this sacred place.

With leaves that flutter, a gentle sigh,
They echo softly, as winds drift by.
Roots stretch wide, through earth they bind,
A promise held by all of kind.

In moonlit nights, the whispers flow,
Of ancient spirits, lost long ago.
Together we stand, both young and old,
In harmony forged, a bond of gold.

The brook sings sweet, its waters bright,
Reflecting dreams in the silver light.
With every turn, a story blooms,
In the heart of the forest, life resumes.

When shadows dance and twilight falls,
The nightingale's song through the silence calls.
Here in the glade, all hearts align,
In the oath of the woods, forever entwined.

Echoes of the Charmed Mirth

In circles round, the laughter grows,
As evening paints the sky with prose.
With every smile, the twilight glows,
Echoes of mirth where magic flows.

From whispered tales of yore untold,
In every heart, that warmth shall hold.
A spark ignites with each sweet cheer,
Charmed and enchanted, our souls draw near.

The stars above, like lanterns bright,
Illuminate dreams that take their flight.
In moonlit dances, shadows play,
As laughter carries the night away.

Through fields of gold, we twirl and spin,
In every moment, we find our kin.
With open arms, the world we greet,
In echoes of joy, our hearts compete.

A tapestry woven in gleeful thread,
Where friendship lingers, and worries shed.
In every heartbeat, magic thrives,
Echoes of a life where joy survives.

Stories Cradled by Petrichor

In vibrant hues after the rain,
The earth awakes, its scent remains.
Stories linger in the mist,
Cradled soft, by nature's kiss.

Each droplet tells of times gone by,
As petals shimmer, the hearts comply.
With every turn of the gentle breeze,
Whispers emerge from the boughs of trees.

Upon the earth, the secrets lie,
Of dreams exchanged, and gentle sighs.
In puddles deep, reflections shine,
Revealing truths, both yours and mine.

The sky dons gray, yet hope still glows,
As wildflowers bloom, in soft repose.
In petrichor's dance, our tales unite,
We wander on through the day and night.

With every storm that sweeps the ground,
New stories rise, and roots abound.
In the heart of nature, we find our way,
Cradled by the earth, we forever stay.

Whispers of the Sylvan Moon

Beneath the veil of a silvery glow,
The woods awaken with secrets to show.
Whispers of night in shadows creep,
Guardians of dreams while the world sleeps.

Stars align in a cosmic dance,
Inviting hearts to take a chance.
In the cool of dusk, the magic hums,
The sylvan moon, where wonder comes.

Through glades adorned in silver light,
The thrill of wonder, a pure delight.
With every rustle, a tale unfurls,
In harmony cast, what magic swirls!

When echoes of silence begin to fade,
And laughter lingers, gently played.
The night unveils a world anew,
In whispers soft, our spirits flew.

In the dance of stars, our hopes align,
Through the canopy, where dreams entwine.
With every heartbeat, the wild things croon,
We're lost forever in the sylvan moon.

The Weaver's Song Beneath the Stars

In twilight's embrace, a loom spun bright,
Threads of silver soft, weaving the night.
Whispers of magic, in shadows they twine,
Fates are entangled, their destinies shine.

Beneath the vast sky, where the dreamers dare,
Stitching the moments with delicate care.
Each star a promise, in needle they flow,
Crafting tomorrows from futures we sow.

The weaver sings sweetly, with each gentle pull,
Creating the patterns that time will extol.
In the quiet of night, her songs softly swell,
Tales of the heart that the shadows will tell.

Around the old trees, the echoes do soar,
Carried by breezes through the open door.
Join in the chorus, let your spirit free,
For the loom spins our stories, eternally.

In a realm of wonder, where night meets the day,
The weaver's enchantment shall lead us away.
In the heart of the stars, all is woven anew,
A tapestry bright, in the heavens so blue.

Ancestral Echoes in Gossamer Light

Through the misty dawn, where the ancient ones tread,
In whispers of time, their soft stories spread.
The roots of the past in the earth's gentle fold,
Hold memories sacred, in silence retold.

In gossamer threads, like the dawn's tender glow,
The spirits awaken, in soft breezes flow.
Echoes of laughter, like bells on the breeze,
Connecting our hearts with the rustle of leaves.

Underneath arching boughs, with grace they entwine,
Ancestral shadows still dance through divine.
In moments of stillness, their wisdom we share,
In the heart of the forest, their presence is rare.

Where the rivers run wild, they've carved out their way,
From the roots to the sky, through night into day.
With every soft whisper that drifts through the air,
We honor their journey, our souls laid bare.

As the sun sets in flames, and the stars start to gleam,
We weave with the past, in a timeless dream.
In the quiet of night, let the echoes be bright,
Guiding our spirits in gossamer light.

Dances of the Celestial Sprites

Amidst the soft glow of the moon's gentle beams,
The sprites twirl in laughter, weaving their dreams.
With glittering wings, and hearts full of glee,
They dance through the night, wild and free.

In the meadows of starlight, with flowers aglow,
Each flicker, a heartbeat, a luminous show.
With whispers of joy, they frolic and play,
Painting the night in a shimmering sway.

Through the branches they flit, a marvellous sight,
Casting long shadows beneath silvered light.
The world holds its breath, as they swirl and spin,
In the dance of the sprites, where magic begins.

Echoing laughter, sweet melodies rise,
The night holds its secrets, concealed from our eyes.
From the depths of the woods to the edge of the stream,
The sprites weave enchantments like threads of a dream.

As dawn stretches forth with a blush on her face,
The sprites take their leave from this enchanted place.
With one final twirl, they blend into the sky,
Bidding farewell with a soft, whispered sigh.

The Echoing Heart of the Sylvan Hollow

In the depths of the hollow, where shadows grow deep,
Soft echoes of nature forever shall seep.
The heart of the forest beats strong beneath,
A symphony whispered, entwining our breath.

In glades filled with wonder, where sunlight does weave,
The secrets of yore in the bark of each leaf.
With murmurs of ancients, the wind does declare,
Stories of love melded with time's tender care.

As twilight descends, the stars start to gleam,
The hollow awakens to night's gentle dream.
Together we gather, united in sound,
For the song of the woods in our hearts will resound.

With every soft rustle of branches that sway,
The essence of magic comes out to play.
In the echoing heart, the wild spirits thrive,
Binding our tales with the pulse of the live.

So listen, dear wanderer, to this sacred space,
Where the echoes of time leave their ethereal trace.
In the sylvan hollow, let your spirit take flight,
As nature's own heartbeat sings softly goodnight.

Glimpses of the Sylvan Realm

In the heart of the whispering trees,
Where sunlight dances with ease,
The shadows breathe in sacred light,
A world awash in pure delight.

With every rustle, tales unfold,
Of ancient spirits, brave and bold,
Their laughter lingers in the air,
A magic hidden everywhere.

The brook hums softly, secrets shared,
Amidst the ferns, the dreams laid bare,
The emerald canopies above,
Cradle stories, pulse with love.

Where fireflies twinkle, a fleeting spark,
Soft footfalls echo in the dark,
Glimpses of a realm divine,
Where nature's enchantments intertwine.

Underneath the luminous sky,
The sylvan whispers softly sigh,
Beneath the moon's soft, silvery gleam,
They weave the fabric of a dream.

Secrets Between Dawn and Dusk

At dawn's embrace, the world awakes,
With dewdrops dancing on tranquil lakes,
The whispers of night begin to fade,
As golden rays in silence invade.

In twilight's cloak, the shadows creep,
While the forest holds its breath, so deep,
Secrets murmur in the gentle breeze,
A symphony of rustling leaves.

The sun dips low, the skies turn warm,
In every corner, a hidden charm,
Birds sing softly, nature's tune,
As day and night commune in June.

Between the hours, magic flows,
In every petal, the wonder grows,
With twilight's kiss, a world feels new,
As stars awaken, dreams come true.

In the balance of light and shade,
Life's secrets shimmer, softly laid,
Between dawn and dusk, we find our way,
A dance of shadows at the end of day.

Prophecies from the Misty Hollow

In the misty hollow, whispers speak,
Of ancient myths and futures bleak,
The fog drapes low, a curtain drawn,
Where hope and fear fuse at the dawn.

A crystal brook, its waters murmur,
While shadows play, and dreams confer,
The echoes of time, they twist and turn,
In hidden nooks, the lanterns burn.

Each step forward, a tale untold,
Of quests embarked and hearts of gold,
With every breeze, a promise glows,
Of paths entwined where magic flows.

Through ancient trees, a vision flows,
Of courage found as the wild wind blows,
Prophecies etched in bark and stone,
Guide the wanderers, never alone.

So linger here, where shadows play,
And watch the skies shift from gray to ray,
In the misty hollow, fate aligns,
With whispers of magic that brightly shines.

Hallowed Ground of the Woodland Fables

In the hallowed ground, where stories lay,
Beneath the boughs where spirits stay,
With every step, the past unfolds,
Of woodland fables, brave and bold.

The ancient oaks, they stand in peace,
Guardians of tales that never cease,
Each rustle a note in nature's song,
Binding us to what feels so strong.

With gentle hands and open hearts,
We weave the threads where wisdom starts,
In twilight glades, the fireflies gleam,
As children of magic chase the dream.

In whispers soft as the evening air,
The woodland fables weave a prayer,
Of love and loss, of brave escapes,
In every shadow, a new tale shapes.

So gather close, let stories share,
The hallowed ground where souls lay bare,
For in each fable, we find our place,
In the heart of the woods, we embrace.

Whispers in the Green Glade

In the heart of the forest deep,
Where secrets in whispers creep,
Leaves murmur tales of old,
In patterns of green, spun gold.

From the branches, soft voices sing,
Of magic in every spring,
Each rustle brings a spark anew,
With the air so fresh and blue.

The brook dances with a tune,
Reflecting the light of the moon,
A lullaby to nature's sigh,
Where dreams of the fairies fly.

Mossy stones cradle warmth and light,
As dawn breaks through the night,
A tapestry of quiet grace,
In this sacred, hidden space.

The winds know all the names of trees,
And carry them gently on the breeze,
While the critters scamper near,
Listening close, intent to hear.

Secrets of the Moonlit Grove

Beneath the silver, watchful night,
The grove glows soft, a mystic light,
Where shadows twine with ancient trees,
And secrets dance upon the breeze.

A whispered vow upon the air,
Of owls and stars, a hidden affair,
The branches bend, secrets exchanged,
In a world where magic's arranged.

Moonbeams filter through the leaves,
Weaving dreams where the heart believes,
Glimmers of light on flowers bloom,
Filling the night with sweet perfume.

Every rustle tells a tale,
Of journeys made through shadowed vale,
Where wishes sometimes come alive,
And hopes awaken, learn to thrive.

In the hush of the midnight hours,
The grove reveals its hidden powers,
A sanctuary for the lost,
In moonlit dreams, we count the cost.

Shadows of the Enchanted Circle

In the circle of ancient stone,
Where magic breathes and groans,
Shadows twist in sacred dance,
A realm where dreams take a chance.

Whispers echo through the night,
Cloaked in the softest light,
Wizards gather, secrets shared,
A legacy of love and dared.

In the stillness, spells are cast,
The echoes of the forgotten past,
Stars align in mystic ways,
Igniting the dark with flame-like rays.

Each heart beats with ancient song,
In this embrace, we all belong,
A bond forged in twilight's glow,
In shadows, our spirits flow.

Let the night consume your fears,
In the circle, shed your tears,
And as the morning breaks anew,
The enchantment wraps around you.

Tales of the Woodland Guardians

Beneath the boughs where silence reigns,
The guardians dwell, free from chains,
With eyes like embers, wise and old,
They weave their tales, both brave and bold.

Each creature holds a story bright,
Of battles fought in the fading light,
Through whispers of the forest deep,
And secrets that the wild ones keep.

With every rustle, tales unfold,
Of friendships forged, and legends told,
The spirits dance to nature's call,
In harmony, they rise and fall.

Every shadow, every beam,
Carries forth a timeless dream,
In the heart of every tree,
Lies the soul of wild, pure glee.

So listen close, as twilight falls,
For the guardians answer nature's calls,
In every breeze and rustling leaf,
They guard the woods, and bring relief.